Gluten Free Cookbook:
Gluten Free Recipes For Healthy Eating

By

Valerie Alston

Table of Contents

Introduction 6

Chapter 1. What to Eat and What Not in a Gluten-Free Meal
.... 7

Chapter 2. Gluten Free Recipes 9

   1. Breakfast 9

      Eggs and Peppers in a Pan for Breakfast...................... 9

      Guilt-Free Gluten-Free Hotcakes 11

      Breakfast Tortilla Recipe 13

      Fluffy Spanish Vegetable Omelette 14

      Delicious Hash Browns.. 16

   2. Lunch and Dinner Recipes... 17

      Chicken and Parmesan Cheese Delight....................... 17

      Creamy and Gluten-Free Pumpkin Pie........................ 19

      Macaroni and Cheese A La Gluten-Free Recipe.......... 21

      Puttanesca Tuna and Pasta 23

      Gluten-Free Pasta Salad... 25

   3. Snacks.. 27

      Toast Cups with Eggs and Crispy Bacon 27

      Avocado and Tomato Gluten-Free Wrap.................... 29

      Crunchy Kale Snacks.. 30

      Extra Sweet Sweet Potato Fries 31

Popcorn with Flaxseed Oil.. 32
Peanut Butter Smoothie with a Chocolate Twist........ 33
Conclusion... 34
Thank You Page... 36

Gluten Free Cookbook: Gluten Free Recipes For Healthy Eating

By Valerie Alston

© Copyright 2014 Valerie Alston

Reproduction or translation of any part of this work beyond that permitted by section 107 or 108 of the 1976 United States Copyright Act without permission of the copyright owner is unlawful. Requests for permission or further information should be addressed to the author.

This publication is designed to provide accurate and authoritative information in regard to the subject matter covered. This work is sold with the understanding that the publisher is not engaged in rendering legal, accounting, or other professional services. If legal advice or other expert assistance is required, the services of a competent professional person should be sought.

First Published, 2014

Printed in the United States of America

Introduction

Gluten free recipes are based on a gluten-free diet, which is a diet that does not allow protein called gluten. You can find gluten in wheat, rye, barley and triticale which is a grain that is a cross between rye and wheat grain. The reason for excluding gluten is that this protein is known to cause inflammation in the small intestine which is seen in people with celiac disease. This diet is thus recommended for people suffering from celiac disease and those with sensitive digestive systems.

If you are used to eating whole wheat and foods that contain gluten then it could be difficult to adjust to a gluten-free meal. But as you use this kind of diet every day, you will find that there may be a lot of foods that you already eat and enjoy that do not contain gluten. And of course sticking to this diet is more than just removing obvious whole wheat foods, rye and barley but you also need to include condiments, beverages and food additives that also contain these ingredients. Eating gluten-free meals will become easy for you and your digestive tract when you follow gluten-free recipes described in this book.

Chapter 1. What to Eat and What Not in a Gluten-Free Meal

In a gluten-free diet you are allowed to eat beans, nuts (provided these are in their unprocessed form), seeds, organic fresh eggs, fresh fruits and vegetables, all kind of meats, poultry and fish (these meats should not be buttered, marinated in sauces or condiments and coated with batter) and almost all kinds of dairy products. You should learn how to read food labels so you will be able to determine which foods contain foods or ingredients found in the unwanted foods list. Be careful of additives and preservatives since most of these may contain wheat and starches.

There are also grains that are allowed in a gluten-free diet; these grains and starches are gentle to the digestive system and thus may be tolerated even by people with sensitive stomachs. Grains such as amaranth, arrowroot, buckwheat, cornmeal, flax seeds, rice flour, corn flour, potato flour, millet, quinoa, rice, soy, sorghum and tapioca are allowed.

You should avoid foods and beverages that contain barley such as malt, malt flavouring and vinegar, rye and wheat. Wheat is also known by so many names like bulgur, durum flour, farina, graham flour, semolina and spelt. Be careful of these foods; you should never drink or eat these unless these are gluten-free-labelled: beer, breads, cakes, candies, pies, cookies, croutons, French fries, gravies, matzo, pastas, salad dressings, sauces, soups, soup bases and so many more.

Chapter 2. Gluten Free Recipes

1. Breakfast

Eggs and Peppers in a Pan for Breakfast

This simple gluten-free recipe uses plain, unprocessed ingredients and are easily available anywhere. You will need about 2 tablespoons of olive oil, 2 medium size onions, a red or green pepper, 2 red chillies, a medium size can of chopped tomatoes, a teaspoon of caster sugar, 4 medium size eggs, a small bunch of parsley, a small cup of plain and thick yoghurt and 2 cloves of garlic.

Prepare the vegetables by washing them beforehand. Cut the peppers and chilies in half, removing the seeds and slicing these into small pieces; chop the parsley into very fine pieces and crush the garlic and chop into very fine pieces. Use a medium size frying pan, heat the olive oil and then sauté the onions, chillies and peppers until these become soft. Add the canned tomatoes and the castor sugar; cook the chilies until the liquid has reduced. Use a wooden spoon or spatula and create four pockets in the mixture; crack each of the eggs open in each pocket. Cook the contents in low heat or until the eggs have set. Place the yoghurt on top and then remove from heat. Garnish the top with parsley and serve right away.

Guilt-Free Gluten-Free Hotcakes

Now you do not have to worry about wanting pancakes even when you have to stick to a gluten-free meal. This recipe uses alternative to wheat flour but it is a guarantee that you will never miss out on the flavour and texture of regular pancakes. You will need about 125 grams gluten-free plain flour, a large egg, about 250 ml of whole milk and butter for cooking the pancakes.

Use a large bowl to mix all the ingredients. Place the flour in the bowl and create a hole in the center of the flour. Crack open the eggs in the center of the flout and then mix with an electric blender or a whisk. When you have managed to create a paste, add half of the milk. Mix these again using the blender and then add the remaining amount of milk. Leave this for about 30 minutes. Stir the mixture just before cooking. Use a medium-size non-stick pan to cook the pancake. Place a small slice of butter; allow the butter to coat the pan just before pouring a small amount of batter. You will know that it is time to turn the pancake when small bubbles have formed on the pancake; when you see these form turn the pancake over. Before cooking another pancake, place another dab of butter over the pan and then pour another amount of batter and then cook the same way. Serve this with butter, agave syrup or with sugar and fruit. This recipe will also work as a waffle recipe; you may add waffle fillings of your choice.

Breakfast Tortilla Recipe

This is a recipe that will provide you with proteins, vitamins and minerals for a delicious, energy-filled breakfast treat You will need about 3 tablespoons of olive oil, 250 grams potatoes with ends trimmed and sliced, a small onion, 2 cloves of garlic, a teaspoon of smoked paprika, ½ teaspoon dried oregano, 3 tablespoons of parsley and 6 large eggs.

You will use a deep 20 cm non-stick pan to fry your tortilla. Place the oil and then fry the potatoes, onion and garlic for 10 minutes or until the veggies are tender. Add the paprika and fry for another minute. Beat the eggs in a medium size bowl together with the herbs and the seasoning. Place the eggs in the pan and then stir as it cooks. Create the tortilla by sliding the mixture into a plate and turning and placing it back in the pan to cook the other side. Garnish the finished tortilla with parsley while it is still hot.

Fluffy Spanish Vegetable Omelette

Spanish food is known to be a combination of hearty meat and vegetables and for a gluten-free breakfast, a Spanish vegetable omelette may be the best recipe yet. You will need about 500 grams of charlotte potatoes, a slice of butter, 2 small size onions, red pepper, 8 large eggs and about 25 grams of chives.

Prepare the vegetables by washing them and scrubbing the potatoes clean. Chop the onions and red pepper finely and set these aside. You will need a medium – sized pan to cook this omelette. Place the piece of butter in the pan and then heat it until it melts gently. Add the chopped onion and peppers and cook these for 5 minutes. Place the potatoes in a steamer and cook over boiling water for 10 to 15 minutes until these are soft enough to press with a fork. Drain it very well and set aside. Place eggs in a bowl and beat with a fork; season this with salt and pepper. Cut the chives into small pieces using a pair of scissors.

Heat your grill and place butter into a pan and add the potatoes. Place the egg mixture over the potatoes and then cook for 10 minutes until these are set and colored golden brown along the sides and underneath. Remove from heat and place the pan over the grill. Cook this for another 2 minutes and then serve when the eggs have hardened.

Delicious Hash Browns

As you may have noticed eggs are a part of almost every breakfast recipe in this article this because eggs are convenient protein sources. You can cook eggs in so many ways plus it may be made to hold different ingredients like in a frittata or tortilla. This hash brown recipe needs 450 grams of waxy potatoes, 350 grams of parsnips, a small onion, a clove of garlic, a large egg beaten and 5 tablespoons of sunflower oil.

Wash the potatoes and parsnips and then grate these in a medium size bowl. You may also use a food processor to grate these into fine bits. Afterwards, grab a mixture and form this into a bowl. Squeeze as much water as you can remove from it and place the ball of mixture back into the bowl. Chop the onion and garlic clove into very fine pieces. Beat the eggs in a bowl. Add the onion, garlic and egg and add salt or pepper to taste. Shape these into small flat cakes (in the shape of hash browns). Heat the oil in a large pan and fry the flat cakes on medium heat for 5 minutes on each side. You can tell that the hash browns are cooked when each side is golden brown in color. Place these on tissue paper to drain the oil. Cook other items in your breakfast menu and serve the hash browns along site these.

2. Lunch and Dinner Recipes

Chicken and Parmesan Cheese Delight

Chicken is a rich source of protein and will provide the body with energy all day long. There may be so many chicken recipes but this one is different; this is tasty, crispy and easy to cook. You will need about 6 ounces of boneless and skinless chicken breasts, black pepper, a dash of salt, a tablespoons of olive oil, 3 garlic cloves, ¼ cup of basil leaves, a juice of a lemon, a cup of gluten-free breadcrumbs, 2/3 cups of parmesan cheese and a gluten-free cooking spray.

Prepare your oven by preheating it to 350 degrees; prepare a large baking sheet where you will cook the parmesan chicken. Season the chicken breasts with salt and pepper on each side. In a medium sized bowl, mix the garlic, lemon juice, basil and olive oil. Place the chicken in this mixture and allow to absorb the mixture for at least an hour. Place the breadcrumbs and the cheese in a the plate. Remove the chicken from the olive oil mixture and then coat these with the cheese and breadcrumbs. Spray the chicken with cooking oil and then bake for about 30 minutes. The best way to bake chicken is hanging it in a cooling rack and baking it. You can tell that the chicken is cooked when its juices run clear as you pierce the chicken with a sharp knife. Serve these as they are or you may cut chicken into bite-sized pieces.

Creamy and Gluten-Free Pumpkin Pie

This is a creamy and rich pumpkin pie with penne made from organic brown rice. You will need salt, a pound of organic brown rice penne noodles, 2 tablespoons of olive oil, a medium onion, 2 cloves of garlic, ½ teaspoon of red pepper flakes, a bunch of kale, 2 cups of vegetable broth, a can of pumpkin puree, a teaspoon of ground cinnamon, ¼ teaspoon of ground nutmeg, 2 teaspoons of yeast, a teaspoon of white wine vinegar, a freshly ground black pepper and about ¼ cup of roasted pumpkin seeds.

Cook the penne noodles in a large pot of boiling water with salt. Reserve a cup of water from the pasta and then rinse pasta from the remaining water. Use a large skillet and heat the olive oil in medium heat. Sauté the onion, garlic, red pepper and cook until the vegetables are needed. When these are ready, add the kale leaves and then cook for another 3 minutes. Add the vegetable broth and the pumpkin puree, cinnamon, yeast, nutmeg and vinegar. Stir this mixture for about 5 minutes. Place the cooked penne pasta into the cooked sauce. Mix these thoroughly and add salt or pepper as needed. Cook for another minute and then add the pumpkin seeds.

Macaroni and Cheese A La Gluten-Free Recipe

There are a few twists to this favourite dish. First of all it uses only gluten-free ingredients and instead of the usual beef or ground pork, shrimps are used instead. You need a gluten-free cooking spray or butter, salt, 8 ounces of macaroni gluten-free, 2 cups of half and half, 2 small sprigs of rosemary, 2 cloves of garlic, 1 pound of shrimp, 4 ounces of soft goat cheese, freshly ground pepper, ¼ cup of bread crumbs gluten-free, ¼ cup of parmesan cheese and a tablespoon of unsalted butter.

Clean shrimps really well, peel of the shell and devein. Crumble your goat's cheese and melt your butter in a pan with low heat. Grate the garlic cloves and grate the parmesan cheese. Prepare your oven to 450 degrees. Spray cups with cooking spray. Boil water and place salt in it to cook the elbow macaroni (follow package instructions). When the macaroni is cooked drain and rinse with running water. Mix the half and half, herbs and garlic in a deep saucepan and then cook this until the mixture boils. Place shredded goat's cheese and then allow the cheese to completely melt. Afterwards, add the shrimp and the well-drained pasta. Cook this for a few minutes until the shrimp has turned pink. When the shrimps are done, divide these into the prepared cups. In a small bowl, combine the breadcrumbs, parmesan cheese as well as the melted butter and mix well. Sprinkle these on top of the cups of macaroni and parmesan cheese and place this in the oven. Bake these for about 10 minutes. You can tell that the dish is cooked by the color of the breadcrumbs; these should be golden brown in color.

Puttanesca Tuna and Pasta

Tuna is a rich source of protein and will definitely be a great source of energy and nutrients. In this recipe you will need a pound of spaghetti gluten-free noodles, salt, two tablespoons of olive oil, 8 cloves of garlic, 6 anchovies in a can, 2 tablespoons of capers, ½ cup of olives, 2 teaspoons of oregano, 1 teaspoon of red bell pepper flakes crushed. You will also ned an ounce of low sodium tomatoes, 2 cans of white tuna in water, 3 cups of organic baby arugula, 2 tablespoons of nutritional yeast as a substitute for parmesan cheese and half a cup of basil leaves.

Prepare the garlic by slicing these thinly, drain the anchovies and the capers, drain the olives and chop into smaller pieces and chop the basil leaves. Cook the gluten-free spaghetti to a boil in heavily salted water. As the noodles are cooking you may now prepare the sauce by heating a large skillet on medium heat. Place the olive oil and garlic and allow to cook for a minute while continuously stirring. Add the anchovies; smash these using the back end of a spoon until these are dissolved. Add the olives, capers, red pepper flakes, tomatoes and oregano. Stir all these ingredients to cook and then add the tuna in water. Allow to boil until the liquid has been reduced for about 10 minutes. Save about ½ cup of starchy water from the pasta. Place the well-drained pasta in the pan and then toss until the pasta is totally covered with sauce. Add the remaining ingredients like the arugula, pasta water, nutritional yeast and the cook until the arugula looks wilted. Just before serving, place basil over the dish.

Gluten-Free Pasta Salad

This is a Mediterranean dish that is easy to make but takes a bit of a challenge to gather all the necessary ingredients. But of course every ingredient is gluten-free and very nutritious. You will need a pound of white rice pasta (elbow shaped), a cup of roasted pistachios shelled, ¼ cup of tahini, 1/3 cup of water, juice of one lemon, a tablespoon of olive oil, a clove of garlic, salt, black pepper, 2 medium-size cucumbers, ½ cup of red onion, a cup of Kalamata olives, ½ cup of mint leaves and about 8 ounces of crumbled feta cheese.

Cook your gluten-free elbow rice macaroni according to package instructions. Place the nuts in a dry and cook over medium heat for about 4 minutes and then cool before you chop into fine pieces. Place the tahini, lemon juice, water, olive oil, garlic and a teaspoon of salt and pepper in a blender; mix these until smooth. Wash and peel the cucumber and chop these into small lengthwise pieces. Remove the seeds and cut into very small sizes. Place these in a large bowl, onion, tomatoes, olives, pasta and the dressing. Use a spatula and toss this mixture until the dressing is evenly distributed. Add more salt or pepper if you wish. Place mint leaves, feta cheese and pistachios when cooked. Place these in the refrigerator if you are not yet going to serve the dish. This is a recipe that will be able to accommodate 10 to 12 people. You may lessen the ingredients if you only plan to make a salad for one.

3. Snacks

Toast Cups with Eggs and Crispy Bacon

This could be a great protein snack for energy during tiring afternoons or could be a perfect breakfast treat for young and old alike since it is very handy to take anywhere. You will need 6 slices of gluten-free bread (be sure to find the label that says so to ensure that you are getting gluten-free bread), 6 slices of turkey bacon or you may also use regular bacon, 6 large size eggs, salt and pepper to taste and red bell pepper cut into flakes.

Use muffin cups to mold bread into cups, spray these with light oil to prevent bread from sticking. Flatten the bread with a rolling pin and then cut the bread into 6 rounds. Place these in each muffin cup but ensure that the bread will look like muffin cups that line the sides of the mold. In a large skillet on medium heat, cook the bacon until these are crispy; it would possibly cook into a crispy piece when cooked for about 5 minutes on each side. Place one piece of cooked bacon on one bread cup and then crack an egg in the middle or over the bacon. Place the muffin bread cups on a baking tray or sheet and bake for 20 minutes. Use a knife to remove the toast from the muffin cup.

Avocado and Tomato Gluten-Free Wrap

This is a very easy snack that makes use of tomatoes, ripe avocadoes and a simple gluten-free snack. This will also work as a breakfast treat for anyone that needs to eat in a hurry. You will need about 4 to 5 tortilla wraps (the best are Ezekiel tortillas) make sure that these are gluten-free, a ripe avocado, a large sandwich tomato, a dash of salt and pepper to taste.

Simply peel the avocado and cut into small cubes. Slice tomatoes into large pieces. Place avocado pieces and tomatoes in tortilla wraps and add a dash of salt and pepper to suit your taste. You may also toast your tortilla wraps to make an extra crunchy snack.

Crunchy Kale Snacks

You may have heard of kale smoothies or kale salad but do you know that there is a cooler way to eat kale and that is to eat these as a snack? Kales are known to be very nutritious and are loaded with vitamins and minerals; therefore you can snack on these kale chips all day long without feeling guilty at all. You will need a large bunch of kale leaves, 3 tablespoons of olive oil and sea salt.

Prepare your oven by heating it to 350 degrees. Wash the kale leaves and remove the ends of the stems. Dry these by covering them in a towel or using a salad spinner to remove excess water. Place individual kale leaves in a baking sheet and sprinkle olive oil on the leaves. Soak the leaves well and then make sure you cover these with coarse salt to enhance its flavor. Bake these kale chips for about 20 minutes. The end results are crunchy and nutritious kale chips!

Extra Sweet Sweet Potato Fries

Sweet potatoes are perfect for breakfast as a replacement for baked potatoes; you may also eat sweet potatoes as snacks by making them extra, extra sweet. You will need 2 medium size sweet potatoes, a tablespoon of brown sugar, 2 tablespoons of olive oil and a dash of salt and pepper.

Rather than frying sweet potatoes in oil, you will bake these in a 450 degree oven. Peel the sweet potatoes, cut these lengthwise and then in half. Line these up in a baking sheet and then sprinkle these with olive oil. In a small bowl combine brown sugar, salt and pepper; mix these thoroughly and sprinkle these on your sweet potatoes. Place the sweet potatoes in the oven and bake these for about 15 minutes. Afterwards remove from oven and turn the sweet potatoes over with a spatula. Place this back into the oven and bake for another 10 minutes. After these are cooked, sprinkle these with salt and serve immediately.

Popcorn with Flaxseed Oil

So you think you cannot eat popcorn any more now that you are in a gluten-free diet? Yes you can when you use an air popper and some flaxseed oil. This popcorn will taste like butter but it does not contain butter at all. You will need a handful of popcorn kernels, a few tablespoons of flaxseed oil, nutritional yeast and salt.

Pop the kernels using an air popper. Once the popcorn is ready, open the lid and drizzle the oil and sprinkle the yeast. Finally add a dash of salt. Mix these completely with the use of a spoon or a spatula. You may make a large batch of popcorn by using two handfuls of kernels but go easy on the yeast.

Peanut Butter Smoothie with a Chocolate Twist

Smoothies are perfect for snacks. This is a peanut butter and chocolate smoothie that will increase your energy during dull afternoons. You will need one frozen ripe banana, about 2 tablespoons of creamy peanut butter, a cup of unsweetened almond milk, vanilla extract, cocoa powder and espresso coffee.

Remove the peel of the banana and chop these into small pieces and place these in a blender. Add the remaining ingredients; you may also have the option of adding espresso coffee or not. Serve with crushed ice or place this in a tall glass with ice.

Conclusion

Going gluten-free is not just a diet but a choice. It is not just a diet for people that have sensitive digestive tracts but also a diet that could help improve your digestion and your elimination. There is no doubt that there are so many advantages of having a healthy gastrointestinal system; one can increase absorption of nutrients, improve immunity, increase release of toxins and help you achieve wellness when you use a gluten free diet.

Finally, going gluten-free will also help you and your family enjoy a variety of foods in their most natural flavors. By eating meals without the use of artificial sweeteners, additives and condiments that are mostly loaded with ingredients that contain gluten, you can appreciate the natural goodness and flavour of foods in the long run. It is true that adapting a gluten free diet is difficult especially for someone that has loved eating sweets and foods that contain gluten but after about two weeks or so, the taste and the flavour will eventually become more tolerable. If you have been diagnosed with celiac disease or you have a sensitive digestive tract then the best diet that you can adapt is a gluten-free diet.

Thank You Page

I want to personally thank you for reading my book. I hope you found information in this book useful and I would be very grateful if you could leave your honest review about this book. I certainly want to thank you in advance for doing this.

www.ingramcontent.com/pod-product-compliance
Lightning Source LLC
LaVergne TN
LVHW021744060526
838200LV00052B/3457